Anne —
He is LORD!,
[signature]
Mt 6.33
4/25/10

LIFE SPEAKS TO US

Thirty Life Lessons Seen Through His Creation

Bill C. Dotson

CrossBooks™
A Division of LifeWay
1663 Liberty Drive
Bloomington, IN 47403
www.crossbooks.com
Phone: 1-866-879-0502

Cover logo design created by Don Crouch.

First published by CrossBooks 02/26/10

ISBN: 978-1-6150-7104-3 (sc)

Library Congress of Control Number: 2009912910

Printed in the United States of America
Bloomington, Indiana

This book is printed on acid-free paper.

Contents

DEDICATION

This book of life expressions is dedicated to my loving wife of over fifty years, Joanne (Gami); my two wonderful daughters, Becky and Evelyn; and my five marvelous grandchildren—Luke, Sarah Peyton, Annie, Will and Renzo. God speaks through each of you daily in my life. I love you all so very much-- Bill, Dad, Bumpa!

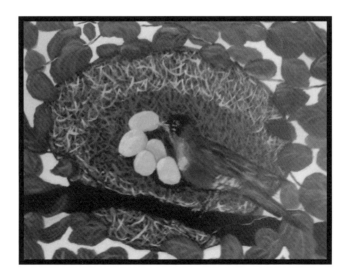

Painting by my eldest granddaughter, Sarah Peyton

ACKNOWLEDGEMENTS

There are always people without whom an undertaking such as this could not happen, or turn out as well. First and foremost, my wife, Joanne, has always encouraged my writing and was the one who bought all the books on self-publishing when she heard this might be a possibility. Sue Jeter, her sister, gave me a book which spurred my interest to actually publish. Jill McPherson, who has spent hours over the past two years molding and shaping the writings into an attractive presentation, and her encouraging words. Jim Williams, who was the first one to tell me I should do these more often and that I might consider doing a book. My daughters, Becky Ellerman and Evelyn Battaglia; for your ideas and encouragement. Three of my grandchildren, Luke, Sarah and Annie Ellerman, who have provided paintings and taken photos, plus being watchful for new subjects for the book. Brad Ellerman, who has presented several good ideas and even helped write one. Steve Owen, for setting up the website, a pre-cursor for the book. All the staff at CrossBooks Publishing who have been a Godsend with all their help. You, the readers over the past two years who have responded with your own stories and exhorted me to do more. But, last and in no ways least, the Source of these reflections, God's Holy Spirit. Through Jesus, He challenged me, opened my eyes to the messages from His creation and gifted me to write and express it. Mainly, He has provided abundant joy to my soul during the journey. For this and much more, thank you. This is your book!

PREFACE TO LIFE SPEAKS TO US

For since the creation of the world His invisible attributes, His eternal power and divine nature, have been clearly seen, being understood through what has been made, so that they (man/we) are without excuse.

-Romans 1.20-

All through my life I have been fascinated by God's creation, marveling for hours over lightning bugs to the moon and stars. Having grown up in a small town in Tennessee, and to have my grandparents' homes be rural farms, I got the chance to see many things up close and personal with most experiences being hands on. And my early childhood was at a time prior to TV. Ducks and chickens, horses, cows and pigs, goats and sheep were a part of life. We had dogs and cats plus all the family hunted and fished, mainly for food. Squirrels, rabbits and birds were a regular at the table while some were reserved as pets.

We captured lightning bugs in a jar and strung large green June bugs by the back leg with thread and flew as a kite. We kept certain bugs and green snakes in our pockets. Frogs were to be handled but beware of the warts they created. Catfish were caught at night along the banks where you swam (skinny dipped) during the day. Poisonous snakes and tarantulas were prevalent and for me, something to be avoided at all cost.

While in the country, candy and other goodies were delivered by a peddler, along with blocks of ice. Refrigeration came along later so we had 'ice boxes' instead. The blocks of ice were placed in a section and it usually kept food from spoiling though not for long. Crops were grown, fresh vegetables were plentiful, hogs and cattle were there to provide meat and milk products. Biscuits were made from scratch, butter was churned, jams and preserves were canned along with certain vegetables. Fruit was grown and dried out for canning on the metal outbuilding roofs. Fried fruit pies were always available. And home made ice cream was churned without the aid of an electric freezer.

The cows were milked by hand, the chickens laid eggs and were gathered daily. Many gave their lives for a tasty fried chicken dinner. The horses were ridden to the blacksmith for 'shoeing'. While some had a name, they were mostly the beast of burden for plowing, hauling and riding, along with the mules and donkeys. I've witnessed cotton being picked by hand, corn and alfalfa being cut and harvested. I helped plow fields as a youngster, behind a mule or on a tractor; picked corn and bailed hay and held calves as they are being neutered. And all of us skipped smooth, round, river rocks across many a creek.

We played marbles in the dirt, compared and traded our special agates. YoYos were big fun and the tricks you learned were awesome. The game of Tittly-Winks was standard along with 'pick up sticks' and 'jacks'. Most boys owned a switch blade knife and we played numerous games of skill with them. Card games and listening to the radio with an imaginative mind were common. Saturday mornings were special. Theaters were called 'picture shows'. Sometimes we spent the entire day watching the westerns several times. The 'good guy' always won. The admission was twelve cents for children. Food, gum and 'cold drinks' (sodas) were pretty well a nickel or less.

All of this and more created in me an awareness that maybe spurred my desire to write about the many facets of life that most of us take for granted each day. The expression 'don't forget to smell the roses' as we move through life is an invitation to observe and marvel at the Lord's creation. And what they say to us is volumes. I especially enjoy reading and memorizing the Psalms since they are so expressive of God's majesty. One particular one may have been the catalyst for leading me to write these short expressions on various subjects and how they each have some life lesson from our Lord. Psalms 19 begins "The heavens declare the glory of God, the firmament shows His handiwork; day after day they pour forth speech; night after night they display knowledge. There is no speech or language where their voice is not heard. Their voice goes out into all the earth, their words to the ends of the world." Thus the title: 'LIFE SPEAKS TO US'. Jesus said He is 'the way, the truth and the *life*'.

I have a passion for the game of golf. It so mirrors the 'game of life' and I am constantly reminded of so many life lessons from it. And since one spends, on average, four hours outdoors, it gives time to observe and reflect. Well, for me, between bad shots. Trees, flowers, cloud formations, animals, water, beautiful terrain and much more are there for the viewing. All are a reminder of who He is and how majestic His creation is. It simply *speaks to us.*

I have written poetry most of my life, primarily for my enjoyment and to bless and pay tribute to special events in my family's life. And as I have progressed in years I have become more keenly aware of His presence and desire to express it to Him and others. In 2008 the Spirit of God prompted me to begin one morning as I was spending time with Him in the word and prayer. Like many things, there was no major plan or an end result in sight; simply the leading and desire to express my thoughts as they came to me. So I started writing and it seemed to flow. As I would send these out to friends, comments would come from a few that encouraged me to do some more. And, now, I find that I have started looking more intently at almost everything each day to see what God might be saying to you and me. Some I write about, some I ponder over. Then, when the Spirit stirs within me, I find He has something to say to me. And I write it down.

Another circumstance probably has impacted my life that led me to this marvelous joy of sensing God's presence is the introduction to what has become, over time, my 'life verse'. It has challenged me to live one day at a time, as best I can through trust in Him. Matthew 6.33 says "But seek first the kingdom of God and His righteousness, and all these things shall be added to you." 'These things" are what we need for a joy filled, abundant and productive life, allowing us to effectively serve Him. And by focusing on today, leaving tomorrow and its needs and issues to itself, we stand a much better chance to 'smell the roses' He has placed in our path.

My hope is that these thoughts will better allow the reader to not miss His glory in everything created; thus, permitting us to worship Him and trust His divine presence and provisions in what He has made, daily. And this way, we see the 'Unseen' through the 'seen'. Truly, "the earth is the LORD'S, and everything in it, the world, and all who live in it." (Psa 24.1) It would be a shame to go through life and miss it/Him. The book has been arranged into a thirty day devotional. My encouragement to you is to read one a day, meditate on the thoughts and verses shown or others you like that amplify the message for you. I prayerfully hope you are blessed through these thoughts and that you will be drawn near to the Creator God.

DAY 1 | *Bushy*

*I*was driving last week and observed a squirrel (we'll call him Bushy) that ran out into the road in front of an oncoming car. He neared the car and, like most squirrels will do, quickly "turned tail" and scooted back to safety to once again, I suppose, attempt to get to the other side of the road. Then, during the day, I noticed several other squirrels in the road that had not been as fortunate as our earlier friend, Bushy.

It got me to thinking. These other squirrels were God's creation, just as much as Bushy. Did God simply love Bushy more than the others? Or, had Bushy just gotten lucky? Was he more skilled at the escape move? Had his parents taught him to be more careful and not play in the street, and his well-equipped mind prepared him to be more observant? Why them and not Bushy? Did God have a better purpose for him?

Then my mind drifted to people. Things, good and bad, happen to us each and every day. Why do some families leave church and get home safely, while others get struck by a speeding motorist who runs a red light and they all die, as happened here in Dallas last week? Why them and not us? Did God not care as much for the family of five as He does for all the others who arrived safely? Why do some of the neatest people die young and others not so neat live to a ripe old age? Maybe our friend Bushy knows since he escaped near death.

Well, I suggest we rely on something a little more substantial than our friend. The Scriptures might be a good place to start. It teaches us that God is omnipresent, omniscient, and omnipotent. This would lead me to believe that Bushy and his other friends were not out of the control of a God this complete. So it must go deeper. The Bible also tells us that He is Divinely Sovereign (Ps 71:16) and Provident (Job 10:12). Simply put, He has a plan for His creation and it is supreme (Jer 29:11). He uses even the bad that happens, created by a sinful, rebellious creation, to fulfill His plan for humanity and the creation He formed. Otherwise, He would not be a God worthy of worship and praise.

He is not asleep or unable to alter circumstances; He simply chooses to work His plan even in light of our disobedience. He has not changed. We have. Most of us know better than to do what Bushy attempted, as there are consequences. But sometimes, we simply do not see the car coming, as is the case of the family of five. What we do have control over is this: trust our lives to the hands of a living, loving God through His Son, Jesus Christ, and be led by His Spirit in our daily walk; knowing "that in all things God works for the good of those that love Him, who have been called according to His purpose" (Rom 8:28). Did we catch that? "according to His purpose"! So relax, it's all in His hands. But Bushy would tell you, please stay out of the street and watch for oncoming traffic!

A few years ago, I was at the eighteenth tee of Bent Tree. I remember it as if yesterday; well, at seventy, probably better. Over to the left at the edge of the first lake were two ducks pecking for food. That is when I notice a third one (we'll call him Quack) gliding into sight; he heads downwind and turns toward the other two. Flaps down, gliding gracefully, descending for a smooth landing. I love to watch and hear them as they swoooooshhh into the water. When you play golf like me, you look for other pleasures. Now for the smooth touchdown. As I watch expectantly, either Quack misjudges the wind or simply hadn't earned his wings yet. He overshoots the water and lands on the bank on his chest (breast, for you purists), tumbles head over duck's feet two or three times, gets on his feet, shakes his feathers, and joins the other two for a time of eating and generally enjoying the day. If ducks blushed, Quack would have been a radiant pink.

You are probably wondering what this has to do with anything spiritual. Okay, here goes. How many of you can honestly say that you haven't laid out the best of plans, with the best intentions, to have them nosedive just like Quack? Your marriage, career, business deal(s), health, just to name a few biggies. We are fallen sinners; we miss the mark. We seek the best wisdom possible, but sometimes none of it produces a smooth, successful landing. Quack will tell you it happens to even the best. Right now, most of you are focusing on Quack's mishap. But that is not the important message he has for you.

What we need to address is how we should react when life seems to slam us into the ground on our chest. What did Quack do? Without hesitation, he jumped to his little webbed feet, smoothed his feathers, and got back in the game. The Spirit, through James, tells us, "blessed is the man who perseveres under trial, because when he has stood the test, he will receive the crown of life that God has promised for those who love Him" (Jas 1:12), and to, "consider it pure joy … whenever you face trials of many kinds because you know that the testing of your faith develops perseverance" (Jas 1:2).

"Stood the test" and "perseverance" really stand out. Quack did, and so can you. Oh, one more thing, and here is the best news, "And the God of all grace, who called you to His eternal glory, in Christ, after you have suffered for a little while, will Himself restore you, and make you strong, firm and steadfast" (1Pe 5:10). Sort of makes the suffering appear worthwhile!

DAY 3 | *Lobster*

While recently vacationing in Chatham on Cape Cod, I encountered the lobster-fishing trade I once had observed in Kennebunk, Maine, as a seventeen-year-old lifeguard and beach boy (pre-George Bush). That is where I learned that clams did not actually originate in the kitchens of Howard Johnson's restaurants. And, I saw firsthand how lobsters were caught in traps in the cold Atlantic waters, a daunting job done by tough men to provide a living for their family and us with a delicacy, which, to me, is unequaled.

This trip, we witnessed the harvesting of the "bottom dwellers," as the catch was brought in and delivered to the clients. We actually saw a reported twenty-pound fellow (Louie), with many others topping the ten-pound mark, not the one-and-a-quarter-pounder we get while dining. Their precious meat is safely encased in a hard outer shell, necessary for its habitat and survival. The challenge of a diner is to crack the shell and enjoy the offering. We all relate the lobster with its claws, never wishing to get our fingers caught in their grasp. The fishermen handle them carefully but efficiently, "'cause that is what they do.'" But I had never focused on the bands they place around the claws. That is when it hit me. No, not the band, I thought.

Once they are all put in a confined tank, they become aggressive fighters, and without the bands to hold their claws together, they would attack and kill each other. They always looked so peaceful staring out of the tank at me. This world and our sinful flesh, aided and abetted by Satan, presses in on us, causing us to strike back, defend ourselves, fight to the finish. God's word is our "bands." He tells us in Scripture that His word constrains (confines, limits, restricts) us. "Your word have I hidden in my heart, that I might not sin against You" (Ps 119:11) .

Louie would tell us that to reach a mature old age, one must persevere through many trials, attacks, even from your own. You cannot believe what Louie endured to reach twenty pounds. We will leave Louie to focus on the similarity to our situation. God uses our trials to provide spiritual growth. Louie did not grow up basking on some sandy beach but on the bottom of a very dangerous ocean, which oddly produced his quality. Same with us.

"No temptation has overtaken you except such as is common to man; but God is faithful, Who will not allow you to be tempted beyond what you are able, but with the temptation will also make the way to escape, that you may be able to bear it" (1Co 10:13). Growing into a mature believer mirrors Louie's trials. As he has a Creator, so do we, one who loves us and has provided His word to aide us through a life of troubled waters. Jesus spoke and lived by the truth, "Man shall not live on bread alone, but by every word that proceeds from the mouth of God" (Mt 4:4). Are you facing your trials alone, without the indwelling of His "true bread," the Word? Then take notice of what God is telling us, "Receive with meekness the implanted word, which is able to save your souls" (Jas 1:21b), and, "He who looks into the perfect law of liberty and continues in it, and is not a forgetful hearer but a doer of the word, this one will be blessed in what he does" (Jas 1:25).

Without the "bands" of God's word in our lives, we, too, are like Louie and his friends in their tank. But with it, the trials in our lives are used by God to produce in us a "delicacy," pleasing to Him and eternally useful for His good pleasure.

Hope you never again look at a lobster the same way. And, check to see if he is wearing bands before reaching in.

DAY 4 | *Ants*

*A*NTS…they're virtually everywhere. Some tiny, others sizable and a few are actually dangerous to one's health, even life. But most of all, they are …BUSY. Wow, are they ever? Have you stopped and just watched them? Do they ever rest? And the loads they carry, many times their size. It must be the six legs. One day there is no sign of them; the next there is a mound of significant proportion. They can travel incredible distances. Ants have been called Earth's most successful species with around 20,000.

Ants are not, to me, pretty, just productive. They are a part of God's creation so they must play a vital role. God even praises them in Proverbs 6.6-8, and tells us lofty humans to "go to the ant, you sluggard, consider her ways and be wise". Men, did you note the 'her'? Well, that may be due to the fact that there are three types in each species; the queen, sterile female workers and males. His <u>only</u> role is to mate with future queen ants and doesn't live very long. A colony may have only one queen, but some may have many. I can see a problem there. They are very social as they communicate by touching each other with their antennae.

OK, they are: hard workers, inhabit almost all the earth, singleness in purpose (finding and storing food), social in nature (some colonies have over a million ants). Sounds like we could learn some great lessons from them. The Proverbs verse continues… "which having no captain, overseer or ruler, provides her supplies in the summer and gathers her food in the harvest". They also hibernate in the winter. God further extols the virtuous ant. "There are four things which are little on the earth, but they are exceedingly wise; the ants are a people not strong, yet they prepare their food in the summer." (Pro 30.24,25)

The ant may have succeeded in her purpose as opposed to us. "God then blessed them, and God said to them, 'Be fruitful and multiply; fill the earth and subdue it; have dominion----over all the earth.'" (Gen 1.28) Unlike the ant, God did not leave us without a captain. He gave us His Son and sealed it with the Holy Spirit. As I see it, He wanted to ensure we would not fail. And the message Jesus left us with right before He departed back to Heaven was "All authority has been given to Me in Heaven and on earth. Go therefore and make disciples of all the nations, baptizing them in the name of the Father and of the Son and of the Holy Spirit, teaching them to observe all things that I have commanded you; and lo, I am with you always, even to the end of the age." (Mt 28. 18-20) The ant would tell us, the ones to whom the command was given –

1) get hard at Kingdom work and

2) fill the earth with disciples through singleness of mind.

You have all the tools and unlike us ants, you even have the power in Christ and His Spirit to succeed.

The next time you think about stepping on an ant, first reflect on the message God has sent us through them. It should make us better Kingdom evangelists and disciple makers.

DAY 5 | *Birds*

*B*irds…countless numbers of them of varying species. In North America alone, there are over 250 birds with their own song, and mating call. Amazing and varied sounds. From the sparrow to the eagle. I am not an official 'bird watcher' but I am fascinated by this member of creation. And let us get it settled up front, once and for all; the male of virtually every class of feathered vertebrates (excludes us men) is the most colorful. Now that we have that settled, let's move on.

So many sayings have passed from one generation to another. Like… free as a bird; birds of a feather stick together; a bird in the hand is worth two in the bush; he/she has birdlike features; you eat like a bird; fly like a bird; a bird nest on the ground; and so on. Man has always been fascinated by flying as he watches the birds seemingly eject themselves from the pull of gravity and soar to heights unknown. I confess I had years of childhood dreams, very real ones, where I flapped my arms and slowly found myself flying, gliding, diving and landing. I can remember today the sense of freedom. Several times I found myself on the floor beside my bed. The diving and landing part I just never mastered.

There is so much they can teach us, but for now, let's focus on 'free as a bird'. This conjures up the impression of release from fear, all is well, a carefree existence. Nothing could be farther from reality. Every bird has a predator enemy, over and above man. They are constantly on the lookout for them. And when they are not paranoid about their surroundings, they are working on a nest, feeding themselves and their young, fighting the elements, and protecting their nest. They hardly rest. Does that sound free to you?

God has a lot to say about birds in scripture, but more on the freedom we have in Christ. True freedom!! We all have our fears. Am I saved, failure, health, marriage, loneliness and many more? Freedom overcomes fear through faith. In Jn 8.31, 32 Jesus says to those that believed in Him (that's faith) "If you hold to my teaching, you are really my disciples. Then you will know the truth, and the truth will set you free". And then in vs. 36 He declares "so if the Son sets you free, you are free indeed". In Lk 13.12 He told the crippled woman; "Woman, you are set free from your infirmity".

Paul stated in Rom 6.18 that "You have been set free from sin and have become slaves to righteousness". Wow, from slavery to sin to slavery to righteousness. Did you hear that? "…similarly, he who was a free man when he was called is Christ's slave. You were bought with a price; do not become slaves of men". (I Cor 7. 22/23) "Though I am free and belong to no man, I make myself a slave to everyone, to win as many as possible."

So to be truly free is, in fact, to be a slave. Figure that one out. Confused? Well, don't be; embrace your slavery to Christ; He paid the price for you, you belong to Him, and the 'freedom' is the ability to rest in Him. Fact: a slave has no rights, he simply belongs to someone who has their best interest at heart and is fully responsible for the love and care of their possession. The birds know this; why don't we? They sing while serving their Creator. And I might add, they do it beautifully in spite of their myriad of issues. In fact, they seem to make a 'joyful noise' to their Creator, one to which I love to listen. Free beings just seem to do it better than the others. So, maybe birds 'really are free' after all.

.

DAY 6 | *Gecko*

$\mathcal{G}$ECKO… no, not the insurance company. Well, they do feature one. And, for sure, research reveals they don't talk, at least not in an Australian dialect. Their name did come from the sound they make. Sort of a gecko sound, I guess. The little tropical lizard-like creatures are all over our backyard. Maybe you have seen them, live and in color; or even multi-color. Mostly green like leaves, or brownish when they are on fences or porches. My grandkids love to net them and place in a container for observation. Sorta man over beast thing. When fearful they show off an orange colored balloon neck. After multiple photo shots, Lizzy is obviously concerned about my interest in her.

They have tiny suction cups called toe pads allowing them to maneuver anywhere at any angle on plants, walls and ceilings. And quickly! The larger species are sometimes kept as pets. They are primarily nocturnal and found mostly in warm climates. Shows they are smart too. And harmless. They have to be a part of the Chameleon family.

Two things catch my attention. First, we, too, are very much akin to Lizzy when it comes to changing colors. Many of us are one thing at home, another at work, at church and for us guys; a whole other person when we get amongst ourselves. I prefer to think of them as masks. Get the picture? At a social setting, or with the boss, I wear one mask. Then woops, I find myself in another setting, displaying a different one. It is at the least tiring, and what about when we drop our guard and find we have the wrong mask on for the occasion. Lizzy will tell you, it's downright frightening to be exposed.

God tells us something about Himself in Mal 3.6a. "For I am the Lord, I do not change;" And the writer of Hebrews reiterated it in 13.8; "Jesus Christ is the same yesterday, today and forever." We are not, but He is. Then on whose strength must we rely for a consistent life and witness? Before we leave this, let's reflect on 'real change'. I Cor 15.51, 52—"Behold, I tell you a mystery; we shall not all sleep, but we shall all be changed, in a moment, in the twinkling of an eye, at the last trumpet; for the trumpet will sound, and the dead will be raised imperishable, and we shall be changed." Now, that's change we can all live with!

Secondly, I can not pass on the orange puffy neck! Lizzy has nothing on us. Paul warns us in Rom 12.3. "For I say, through the grace given to me, to everyone who is among you, not to think of himself more highly than he ought to think, but to think soberly, as God has dealt to each one a measure of faith." In Hab 4.2 the prophet says "See, he is puffed up; his desires are not upright – but the righteous shall live by his faith." God is calling us to live by faith in His attributes, not to rely on or flaunt ours. What a relief, and at the same time an equal challenge.

If you are like me, I love being with someone that simply is him/herself in whatever setting. How refreshing. They are confident and satisfied with who they are. It really is disarming and certainly comes across. The expression fits. 'What you see is what you get.' We, as Christians, for all the reasons, should be just that; content 'in Christ'. "God forbid that I should glory (boast), except in the cross of the Lord Jesus Christ, by whom the world has been crucified to me, and I to the world." (Gal 6.14)

DAY 7 | *Snow*

*S*NOW… water vapor in the atmosphere that has frozen into ice crystals and then falls to the ground in the form of flakes. Beautiful to most, but a hazard to many. I confess, I love it. Kids of all ages await the first snow. All the many games; skiing, sledding (made from anything that will slide), building snowmen, some very creative. And always, snowball fights. Snow cream was my favorite as a kid. And how else could Santa's sleigh get from the North Pole without it? Snow covered mountains are so breathtaking.

It is believed that no two snowflakes are alike. Have you ever examined them closely? Brilliant designs of thin crystals, reflecting and refracting light. Catch them on a cold mirror or glass. You'll be fascinated. Many songs have been inspired by snow and the season. Especially around Christmas time. So peaceful. Especially while it is falling with a hot brewed drink and a cozy fire. 'Let it snow, let it snow, let it snow!!'

The uniqueness of each flake is what catches my attention. Just like every human that has or ever will live; a specific DNA, with none alike. The iris in the eye and fingerprint of each individual is unlike anyone else. Trust me; I watch Law and Order. God's word is a better source. Psa 139.13-16 tells us in part "..I am fearfully and wonderfully made….my frame was not hidden from You when I was made in the secret place….” “Your hands made me and fashioned me.” (Psa 119.73a)

God told Jeremiah in 1.5a “That before I formed you in the womb I knew you..” and Isaiah 44.24a shouts at God's unique fashioning of man. “Thus says the Lord, your Redeemer, and the one who formed you from the womb; I, the Lord, am the maker of all things..” And the marvelous part is revealed in the Creation accounts when God looked on everything He had made and declared it 'very good'. (Gen 1.31a) We have a friend in Nashville who states that 'God don't make no junk'. And he is right. Just as each flake of snow is unique and beautiful, so are we.

You say, but we sure don't appear and act beautifully. And many are born with forms of disabilities. Well, sin and its influence have had a significant impact on each of us. That is why He reminded Isaiah that He was his Redeemer. In Christ, the Father sees us as we were intended and will one day become. Just as we can see the snowflakes in all their beauty, so God sees us as fully redeemed and dressed in the robes of Christ. He even says He has a new name for each of us. Rev 2.17b is a glorious promise to 'those that overcome'. “I will also give him a white stone with a new name written on it, known only to him who receives it.” Talking about UNIQUE!!! And it is eternal. Can't wait. How about you?

Got any snow stories? Just hop on your sled, come on over and we'll reflect together. You might wait till it actually snows.

STARS…not the ones in Hollywood, but those celestial, burning lights in the sky, visible on most nights as they sparkle brilliantly for all the world to see. Some seem to just be out there in space all alone, detached from us and anything else. And then there are those clustered into shapes and images with names. Orion, Leo, Cancer, Pegasus, Ursa Major and Minor; constellations of great magnitude, just to name only a few of the 88. On a clear night recently in Hilton Head, SC away from the city lights, they seemed to be right on top of us. The naked eye sees only a small number in our galaxy, but at observatories, the world out there opens up to incredible proportions. In August, the best month, we sometimes just lie back, looking skyward along the horizon, and observe the shooting stars (meteors) racing through the Earth's atmosphere to their ultimate destiny. And all of us (at least Texans) have sung 'the stars at night are big and bright, deep in the heart of Texas.'

Scientists continue to discover galaxies beyond ours. How vast is the Universe? One source reported in 1999 that 'The Hubble Space Telescope has found there may be 125 billion galaxies in the universe.' The number of stars is countless, maybe 200 billion times more than the grains of sand on Earth. And we are told in Scripture that each has a name known only by God. He named them all. Now why would He do that? Well, I have a theory that if we were the Creator and we made something very special, we might just 'name it'. The real question should be, why not? In Genesis He proclaimed the moon, sun and stars to be good, pleasing to Him. They each are precious in His sight. And He made plenty of them. On the other side of this earthly veil, I bet we will get to see them all and learn their names, and what purpose each serves.

I like the fact that they draw us heavenward. It is just plain worshipful. "The heavens declare the glory of God…" (Psa 19.1a) How can anyone pause and gaze at them and not ponder the greatness of God's universe? The Psalmist uses the word 'declare' to describe the manner in which the stars, planets and the heavenly galaxies pronounce His nature and eternal power. And God dwells in this sanctuary of unequaled splendor. "When I consider Your heavens, the work of Your fingers, the moon and the stars which You have ordained, what is man that You are mindful of him…" (Psa 8.3/4a) The Psalmist has it right—everything in the creation is so marvelous, how does He even have time for us? But He does!!

In fact, He thinks so highly of us (man) that "He has made man a little lower than God, and has crowned him with glory and honor. He has made him to have dominion over the work of His hands, and placed all things under His feet…" (Psa 8.5/6) Wow!! Talk about privilege, and responsibility! And when the 'Owner' turns over His creation to His caretakers (us), doubtless He trusts us to do an excellent job, but more than that, He has not left us alone to stumble and fail. He promised "to never leave you or forsake you"—"and, lo, I am with you always, even to the end of the age." (Heb 13.5b & Mt 28.20b)

What part of His creation has He placed under your care? What arena does He have you in? Who or what are you responsible for? Are you a single star or are you a part of a larger constellation here on earth? How are you measuring up to the tasks with which He has entrusted you? Are you as obedient to His commands as the stars? Jesus said in John 21 'tend my lambs, shepherd my sheep, tend my sheep'. Like the stars and the other parts of creation, as recorded in Gen 1, He declared it 'very good' when He looked upon His creation and man, "making us in His own image.." And just what is your 'image of God'? Is it one that can't seem to measure up to your daily issues, one that appears distant and uninterested, who just doesn't understand your difficulties and trials? Or is His image that of a Creator that placed all the stars in the myriad of galaxies and gave each a name and purpose, and yet is so interested in your well-being that He stooped down and died on a cross, rose from the dead and has promised you eternal life, now and forever, if you, by faith, would trust Him? For salvation and your life here on Earth.

And how can you gaze at a star laden sky and do anything but trust Him? They simply 'declare His glory'. And His Son, Jesus, is that 'ETERNAL STAR' that we will one day gaze upon for eternity. In Rev 22.16 we hear Jesus say "I, Jesus, have sent My angel to testify to you these things for the churches. I am the root and the offspring of David, the bright morning star." So, the next time you look heavenward, proclaim with the Psalmist—"The earth is the Lord's and the fullness thereof, the world and they that dwell therein." (Psa 24.1) That's worship in its truest sense and what He truly desires is our worship and praise. "Let everything that has breath praise the Lord. Praise the Lord!" (Psa 150.6) A star studded universe simply helps us do just that. But lest we forget, our worship is of the Creator, not His creation.

Afterward, shoot me a starry thought about God's message to you.

DAY 9 | *Mammon*

*M*ammon... material wealth with an evil influence. You know it today as money, riches, or possibly filthy lucre. If this is true, why in the world do we pursue the stuff with intense passion? God stated that no one can serve Him and Mammon/Money. He calls the two, Masters, in Mt 6.24.

We go to school, try to excel, get the highest paying job. Nothing wrong with that. Some use honest means to accumulate it. Sounds okay to me. But some use deceitful or dishonest ways to get as much as possible. They want their share and ours too. And when does enough become enough? When we have more than our friends, neighbors, club buddies or even our parents, especially dear ole dad. The bumper sticker tells it all for many... 'THOSE WHO FINISH WITH THE MOST TOYS WIN!' But do they?

The true word for it is GREED! Driven by self-centeredness. Hunger for power from the accumulation and use of wealth. Social status purchased at the price of, maybe, your soul. What we see happening today across the world, the financial meltdown it is being called, has revealed the very worst in man. You see it in business, financial markets, government, sports, Hollywood and, yes, even religious institutions.

So, what does the word of God, the only infallible rule of faith and practice say? In Mt 13.22b, Jesus talks about 'the deceitfulness of wealth'. The rich young man "went away sad because he had great wealth". (Mk 10.22b) Jesus offered him eternal life. He chose Mammon. James, in 5.2/3, tells the rich oppressors that "your wealth has rotted… you have hoarded wealth in the last days".

I Tim 6.9/10 get to the heart of the matter. "People who want to get rich fall into temptation and a trap and into many foolish and harmful desires that plunge men into ruin and destruction. For the love of money is a root of all kinds of evil. Some people, eager for money, have wandered from the faith and pierced themselves with many griefs." The key is 'the love of money'.

Proverbs 10.22 tells us a different story. "The blessing of the Lord brings wealth, and He adds no trouble to it." Wow, Lord, give me some of that. Mt 6.33 sets it straight. "Seek first the kingdom of God and His righteousness, and all these things (necessities for joyful living) will be added unto you." See, it's not the 'wealth', it's the consuming fire of the love for it. And it matters not whether you have it or simply desire to have it. The 'evil influence' creates for many an idol to be worshipped and relied upon for self worth and security. Test yourself right now; where is your true security?

That is why He tells us to hold it loosely, as it is fleeting and deceptive. He, our true Master, on the other hand, is not. And the unexcelled joy is; when we are pursuing Him, and He chooses to add levels of wealth to us, He also gives us the desire to serve Him with it. "… store up for yourselves treasures in heaven, where moth and rust do not decay/destroy." (Mt 6.20a) This way, we can avoid the sticky finger syndrome.

And if you are struggling with excess Mammon, call me. My friends and I are experiencing the 'financial meltdown'.

| *Mercy*

$\mathcal{M}$ERCY…is the name given to the little fellow shown here. Recently, we arrived at our grandchildren's home here in Dallas, to find two small ducklings scampering across the street, with no mother in sight. No older than a week, you should have seen them maneuvering the curb. After a very long chase we finally cornered them and took them inside, hoping to see their mother show up soon. But, alas, no one came. After a feeding, some water and a container for a rest, they nervously settled in. Names were given; Goodness and Mercy. Goodness was not well and lived only a day. Sadness prevailed. Mercy is still with us. Growing and thriving from the wonderful care being given. It has even been on a long road trip.

As I was thinking about Mercy this weekend, it reminded me that this is exactly what God has shown us. Mercy did not even have a name till it was found and taken in. Known only to God, it was left alone to fend for itself. No sense of direction, simply lost. But, like Mercy, we were drifting, lost and homeless. Fortunately for this little duckling, it fell into the hands of a loving family that took it in and cared for it, nourishing it.

What would Mercy tell us about mercy? I was lost, in need of help, and someone took me in. I was hungry and they fed me. And you can't get more 'least' than me. I have no role models so the family is showing me how to be a duck. There are two big dogs; I'm talking huge, that could have me for a quick snack, but the girls created this home for me that is safe from 'them'. I don't need clothes it appears, but I bet they would give me some if I needed them. The family is Christian and I've heard them speak of God, our Creator. And something about Matthew 25.35-36.

They say this is about showing mercy. And if you give mercy, you get some back like Matthew wrote in his letter around 5.7. I don't know my father, but they keep talking about "being merciful, just as your Father in heaven". Luke is the eldest boy in this family and he evidently wrote a letter, too. 6.36 is the verse they talked about. The Bible must be a great book for humans. You hear them talking about it all the time. You know, we ducks don't have one for us. What a shame. So what does my name mean?

Mercy…charity, clemency, compassion, forbearing. In James 5.11b we are told "the Lord is full of compassion and mercy". And when it is Divine mercy, it lasts for eternity. Simply not getting what you deserve. It is best understood when one is dispensing it. And my two granddaughters are truly dispensing it, big time. I believe Mercy knows it and so does our Heavenly Father. And the two blind men along the road knew it also. They cried to "Jesus, Son of David, have mercy on us". Twice they shouted. Jesus stopped and called them. "What do you want Me to do for you?" "Lord, we want our sight". "Jesus had compassion on them and touched their eyes. Immediately they received their sight and followed him." (Mt 20.29-34)

If you have trusted Christ as your Savior by grace through faith, then you too understand the incredible depth of mercy. The cross where He suffered and died for you and me is explanation enough. If you have not experienced it, Mercy would ask you 'what is holding you back'? Jn 5.24 says it best.

Soon, Mercy will grow some feathers, and it will be time to place it back into its natural environment, having been a recipient of loving mercy from a family who has received mercy. Let's all go and do likewise.

I know many of you have shown or received mercy this way. Let Mercy and the kids hear from you.

DAY 11 | *Tears*

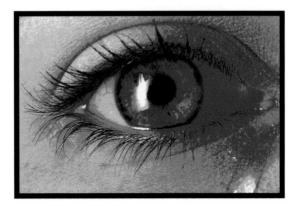

*T*EARS…are simply water fluids. So, what is the big deal? They come from normal secretion to clean and lubricate our eyes right through the lachrymal glands (weep holes) our Creator designed for us. Crying simply increases the flow. Babies cry a lot usually because of discomfort. There are many subtle and distinct causes. Some are dejection, excitement, lamenting, necessity, pain, pity and relief. It's just like a loving God to think of this for our well-being; physically and emotionally.

James Dobson tells a story of a mother who reported an event with her children. Her young daughter and the baby were left on the floor in his room. Deafening silence broke forth and mom became concerned, so she went to the baby's room to find no one. She ran down the hall and found them in the girl's room. Mom scolded her. 'You were told to never carry your baby brother.' With huge crocodile tears flowing down, she replied; 'but mom, I didn't disobey, I rolled him'. How can you stay mad at that?

Weddings and funerals. Killers! First baby, separation, fear, reconciliation, state championship, Dear John letter, graduation, promotion, sweet note, sad movie, new puppies. Add your list. Emotions run the gamut. One minute I'm crying with joy; the next I'm hit hard by sadness. A roller coaster, and tears accompany them all!

The expression; 'big boys don't cry' or 'real men don't cry' is such a lie and debilitating to any male. It simply is counter intuitive to all that God intended. Let's see some of what He tells us in Scripture. Now Job was a man's man I would think. In 16.20,21 Job prays "My intercessor is my friend as my eyes pour out tears to God; on behalf of a man he pleads with God as a man pleads for his friend". And King David, no wimp of a man, cries out to God throughout the Psalms. "I am worn out from groaning; all night long I flood my bed with weeping and drench my couch with tears." (6.6) "My tears have been my food day and night, while men say to me all day long, "Where is your God?"" (42.3) David was a crier, big time, and he was "a man after God's own heart". What does that tell you?

And ole Peter, 'The Rock' on whom Jesus was to build His church. Surely not him also. But we find in Mt 26.75b; after he had denied Jesus three times and the cock crowed the last time; remembering Jesus' words earlier, "he went out and wept bitterly".

While there are many, there is certainly one more. The Man of Men, the King of Kings. Fully God, fully man; "Jesus wept", as he had compassion on his friends who were weeping as they grieved over Lazarus, Jesus' friend. (Jn 11.35) In vs. 34b we see "He was deeply moved in spirit, and was troubled". Mary, Lazarus' sister, was there. She had earlier washed His feet with her tears and her hair. And when He looked out over Jerusalem during His last week on earth, even as his followers were rejoicing, doubtless many crying for joy of seeing the Messiah, we are told "He saw the city and wept over it". (Lk 19.41b) He wept for friends and for the city, but finally for the world He came to save. Lk 22.44 reflects His ultimate struggle. An angel from heaven was sent to strengthen Him because of the pain. "And being in agony He was praying very fervently; and His sweat became like drops of blood, falling down upon the ground."

And for you and me, He gives us the formula for living victoriously in Psa 126.5,6. Not what we would expect. "Those who sow in tears will reap with songs of joy. He who goes out weeping, carrying seed to sow, will return with songs of joy, carrying sheaves with him." WOW!! And He said "I tell you the truth, you will weep and mourn while the world rejoices. You will grieve, but your grief will turn to joy." (Jn 16.20)

So, we see clearly tears are many times necessary, for a multitude of reasons; and acceptable, even pleasing, to our Lord. Don't hold back (okay, men?)! Our Lord didn't. But one day He promises "He will wipe away every tear from their (our) eyes; …. there shall no longer be any mourning, or crying, or pain.." (Rev 21.4) Allelujah!!!

Clear your eyes and send me your thoughts. We'll cry together.

DAY 12 | *Blood*

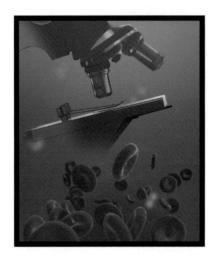

*B*LOOD…is the agent of life. It is red, while some folks claim to be 'blue blooded'. It owes its color to hemoglobin, a respiratory protein containing iron in the form of heme, to which oxygen binds. Human blood is a liquid tissue. Its major function is to transport oxygen necessary to life throughout the body. It also supplies the tissues with nutrients, and contains various components of the immune system defending the body against infection. Several hormones also travel in the blood.

It moves in blood vessels and is circulated by the heart, a muscular pump. It passes to the lungs to be oxygenated, and then through the body by arteries. It diffuses its oxygen by passing through capillaries; then returns to the heart through veins. It also transports metabolic waste products, drugs and foreign chemicals to the liver to be degraded and to the kidney to be excreted in urine. Wow, must have been a Divine Creator that designed this complex circulatory system. I am not sure a 'big bang' could have pulled this off.

Like many of you 'red blooded' folks, I have the privilege of donating whole blood every 60 days. When this happens, I am reminded of the value of blood for the life and health of humans. Each of us has about a gallon in our body at all times. Doesn't seem like much, but it is what provides life. In wars, blood is shed for the defense of a nation and its people. I can lose my hair, maybe an eye, or tooth, finger, a leg, kidney and certain other body parts without losing my life. But not blood.

When I was a boy, I fell on an exposed scooter handlebar that went into the front of my skull. My Mother heard me screaming and saw me running with blood streaming out of my head. Another time I fell on a milk bottle I was carrying and it severed my wrist and several arteries. Fortunately, in both instances, we made it to the hospital and my life was saved, not without a severe amount of blood loss. Truly, I experienced firsthand that life is in the blood.

Scripture shows us the importance of blood, as it relates to sin, forgiveness and sacrifice. From the beginning, after our first parents sinned, God made the first blood sacrifice recorded in Gen 3.21 where "God made tunics of skin and clothed them". God covered them with the skin of a sacrificed animal. All through the Old Testament we see countless examples of the vital issue of shed blood. God's covenant with Abraham was consummated in Gen 15 by God walking between the halves of a goat and ram while Abraham slept. Blood had to be shed to seal the covenant.

One of the most telling scriptures in the Bible is recorded in Lev 17.11. "For the life of the flesh is in the blood, and I have given it to you on the altar to make atonement for your souls; for it is the blood that makes atonement for the soul." The blood sacrifices described in Leviticus are the precursor of the eventual perfect sacrifice of Jesus at Calvary. And the dietary laws for Israel required that meat should be drained of blood (life) before eaten. "But you shall not eat flesh with its life, that is, its blood." (Gen 9.4) So much of God's eternal plan centers around the subject of blood.

The Covenant with Israel through Moses and the Ten Commandments was sealed by blood. In Ex 24. 4, "And Moses wrote down all the words of the Lord. Then he arose early in the morning, and built an altar ….for the twelve tribes of Israel". In vs. 6, Moses took half the blood and put it in basins, and the other half of the blood he sprinkled on the altar.' And vs. 8 concludes; "So Moses took the blood and sprinkled it on the people, and said, 'Behold, the blood of the covenant , which the Lord has made with you in accordance with all these words.'"

While the priests used the firstborn and perfect animal sacrifices to atone for sin(s), it was only when God chose to send Jesus, His first and only Son, to make the ultimate sacrifice as a propitiation for mankind's sins that we received redemption, once and for all. While Christ was hung on a cross to suffocate, scripture was fulfilled and atonement was made when the soldiers pierced Him in the side and His blood, along with water, flowed from Him. He ushered in the 'new covenant'. "Likewise He also took the cup after supper, saying, 'this is the new covenant in My blood, which is shed for you.'" (Lk 22.20)

Our blood should have been shed; we should have drunk the cup Jesus drank. But that would not have satisfied the Father. Just like He made the covenant with Abraham, He was the only one who walked between the slain animals, and His Son was the only one who could die for sin. See, eternal life is only in Jesus' perfect blood. Simply put, God made both covenants with Himself because He knew He is faithful and we are not. And both were sealed with blood. He gave us His blood (His life) when all we really deserved was death. Sounds like AMAZING GRACE to me!!

The next time you prick yourself and bring blood, think on Jesus and His glorious sacrifice. He is worthy!

DAY 13 | *Trees*

*T*REES...one of the parts of creation that fascinates me. Tall ones, fat ones, skinny ones fruit bearing ones, old ones and new ones. (sounds like people) Some are majestic, some brilliant with color; while others are simply green and fill a space. Each has its own life cycle, mainly depending on the type and its ability to access water to survive and grow. One of my favorites is the Pecan just behind the 15th green at Bent Tree CC. It sits up high and towers over the rest. Its real beauty is its trunk and limbs, which show the years it has survived the storms, somewhat crooked and gnarled as it rises into the air. It's sorta grandfathery! I hope it outlives me.

The Aspens, the Smokeys, Vermont, Yellowstone, northern California; each conjure up thoughts of trees of every nature. Breathtaking size, or color or both. Each year people travel extensively to just see them, and the changing of the colors. My favorite was going to Knoxville each football season for the TN/AL game in mid October, and then at times, on up to Gatlinburg in the Smokeys.

Birds rest or nest in them; squirrels and monkeys love playing in them. Kids climb them, we build houses in and from them; we seek shade from the sun under them. We eat fruit or nuts from them. We stay warm from fires built from their limbs; while most of us just admire them.

Have you noticed how most tree limbs reach skyward, as if they are lifting their arms in praise and worship to their Creator? And the ones that grow tallest and endure longest are located near streams of water. The Psalmist uses a metaphor of a tree and streams to show the need for spiritual growth and the result of their relationship; the word of God being the streams of living water. (Psa 1.3)

Gen 2.9 tells us… "And the Lord God made all kinds of trees grow out of the ground – trees that were pleasing to the eye, and good for food." And the command to be obedient in the Garden involved the "tree of life" and the "tree of knowledge of good and evil". In Rev 22.2b, we see that the tree of life is spreading over each side of the river in the new Heaven, bearing much fruit and are for the healing of the nations.

Be reminded that God chose to use a tree from His creation to demonstrate the greatest act of love in all of history, at Calvary. A tree was cut down that Jesus might be lifted up.

In Isaiah 61 the prophet declares the "year of the Lord's favor". Jesus, the Savior, is announced to the nations. And you and I, recipients of His favor, are called 'oaks of righteousness'. Trees are very significant in God's design of life, both temporal and eternal. Next time you find yourself gazing at an interesting tree, let your thoughts drift to praise for the One Who made it. They are everywhere, so you don't have to go far to revel in amazement and worship. You might even be very un-Presbyterian and lift your arms skyward, just like the tree. And shout.. "the heavens declare the glory of God, and the firmament shows His mighty works"; behold I am an 'oak of righteousness'. Check first to see if anyone is watching.

DAY 14 | *Sandy*

*H*ave you ever met a Bearded Dragon that you did not like? Truthfully, I have only known one. He belongs to Sarah Peyton, my oldest granddaughter. He (I guess) is nearly three years old, and his name is Sandy. Sandy is very fortunate to have her as his care giver.

This agamid lizard is native to Australia. They are affectionate, with a calm and gentle nature, with broad, triangular heads and flattened bodies. Remind you of anyone you know? They reach 18-24" head-to-tail and typically live 8-15 years. When threatened, they will expand a tiny pouch under their jaw, inhale air and puff up to make them appear larger. The pouch resembles a beard; thus their name. The two Aussie golf pros at Bent Tree call them 'frill necked lizards'. They have a hard shell exterior and a soft belly. Sandy eats carrots and crickets (quickest tongue in the west), and boy are his tiny claws sharp. When he is out, he is usually resting on her shoulder or lap.

As I observed him wrapped in a white washcloth after a bath, I reflected on Sandy to her dad. Being a quick witted chap, Brad exclaimed, 'in spite of his rough exterior, he is well loved. Same with us and God.' You know, he is right. To us, Sandy is bascially an ugly critter. But to Sarah, he's anything but. Which leads me to us. The scripture says "there is none righteous, no not one". (Rom 3.10) And that we were actually God's enemy. (Rom 5.10a) Which begs the question; how can anyone unconditionally love an unrighteous enemy? For most Americans, Osama bin Laden comes to mind.

Are we that different from Sandy? As a single example; when confronted, have you ever 'puffed up' to appear more powerful than you are? To get your way. I do, way too much.   It's just plain ugly. In Hab 2.4 the Spirit tells us that man "is puffed up; his desires are not upright, but the righteous shall live by his faith".   Sandy puts his whole faith in Sarah. It's truly a beautiful relationship. Our beauty is in the righteousness of Christ. Outside Christ, we are a whole lot uglier than Sandy. "The righteous shall live by faith in the Son of God." (Gal 2.20) That would be Jesus! God does not see us in our ugly, pitiful state if we are 'in Christ', but we are viewed through His Son whose obedience (faith) was demonstrated in His life, death and resurrection. Remember the white cloth wrapped around Sandy? Points to what we will receive in Glory. White robes of righteousness (Rev 7.9). No more ugliness!!!   The word for this transformation is GRACE!!!

What about you? Got any 'critter' stories?

DAY 15 | *Salt*

$\mathscr{S}$ALT… is an interesting condiment most of us take for granted. It is a crystalline compound (NaCl) that consists of sodium chloride. It is abundant in nature. There are several names given to it for various uses: common salt, mineral salts, and smelling salts. Most of us relate it to the common table salt. There is Kosher and Rock salt. I am especially familiar with the latter as my family loves homemade ice cream. Salt is used in numerous expressions such as..a pinch or grain of salt, salt of the earth, worth one's salt. Sailors are referred to as 'old salts'.

It is especially used to season and/or preserve food. Having grown up in my early years in rural Tennessee, I observed 'hog killing time'. (Sorry, ladies-and we won't discuss the sausage) Families had 'smokehouses' where they hung hams and bacon for curing before eating during the ensuing year, or selling to the market. Salt was rubbed over the raw meat, primarily to preserve the meat from the atmosphere and flying insects, but at the same time it was adding an appetizing flavor.

In Israel, salt entered largely into the religious services of the Jews as an accompaniment to the various offerings presented on the altar. I found it interesting that God provided them with an inexhaustible and ready supply of it on the southern shores of the Dead Sea. As one of the most essential articles of diet, salt symbolized hospitality; as an antiseptic, durability, fidelity and purity. Hence, the expression ..'Covenant of Salt'. Lev 2.13; Num 18.19; 2 Chron 13.5. "…with all your offerings you shall offer salt".

In Mk 9.50 Jesus makes a statement, provides a warning and exhorts us. "Salt is good, but if the salt becomes unsalty, with what will you make it salty again? Have salt in yourselves and be at peace with one another." He also said in Mt 5.13…"You are the salt of the earth". And in Col 4.6 Paul exhorts us to make the most of every opportunity to the non-believer. "Let your speech always be with grace, seasoned, as it were, with salt, so that you may know how you should respond to each person."

Most chefs know how to add just the right amount of salt to excite and satisfy the palate. Too little, it is bland and tasteless; too much, it dominates and makes it undesirable. If Jesus has pronounced us to be 'salt of the earth', then it is within our power to be a preservative for His Kingdom and make it so flavorful and attractive to the unbelieving world, they will be unable to resist 'tasting Him for themselves'. As Christ's chefs, let us be that flavorful preservative that God has called you and me to be….both in our relationships with Believers and non-believers. And just as in Israel's offerings, we too have an endless supply of 'salt'. We get it not out of a dead sea, but from a Living Lord, through His word, prayer, fellowship and abiding in the Spirit.

Next time you pick up a salt shaker, be reminded of who you are in Christ.. 'the salt of the earth'. Check your shakers and make sure they're full (not to stay that way, but to be emptied out on a needy world).

DAY 16 | *Ghosts*

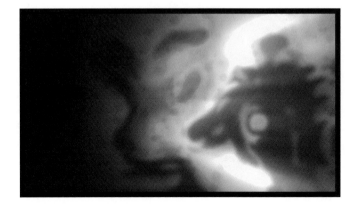

$\mathscr{G}$HOSTS…conjure up a myriad of thoughts, mainly eerie and mysterious. Most are perceived differently than Casper, the friendly ghost. I'm talking the kind in Ghost Busters, and in A Christmas Carol by Charles Dickens (1843). Scrooge is visited by his former partner, Marley. Deathly appearance, in chains and plain scary. Fear grasps Scrooge by the neck and he experiences suffocation. That's primarily what ghosts are supposed to do. INVOKE FEAR!!!

It is 2009, and during the previous year, many, if not all of us, started facing the haunting presence of fear, maybe as never before. Have you ever sat around a fire at night and told 'ghost stories'? None are real, but the perception and our imagination start to capture our minds. Some become 'frightened to death', so to speak. Simply, fear takes over. So, what is this deadly enemy of peace? Well, the negative side is apprehension, terror, dread, anxiety caused by the actual or perceived nearness of danger, evil or pain.

For most of us, it is misguided thoughts about the future, without any application of faith. To me, there are two distinct sides of fear. So, how do I move to the other side when I am scared of what might happen? First, I have experienced throughout life that most of my fears were not well founded. But how can we always know which ones are or are not? We usually can't! That is where the application of faith takes hold. Just listen to how scripture defines faith. In Heb 11.1 we learn that "faith is being sure of what we hope for, and certain of what we do not see". Faith acknowledges the future unknown. But its foundation on which one stands is being sure, hope and certainty. Well, you say, I am certain all these bad things are going to happen to me and I am fearful. Maybe some will. But as the saying goes, 'the greatest fear is fear itself'.

Scripture confirms that some bad things will happen. That is why God asks us to trust Him with the future and our misplaced anxieties. "Cast your cares on the Lord, and He will sustain you; He will never let the righteous fall." (Psa 55.22) In I Pet 5.7, He tells us again to "cast all your anxiety on Him because He cares for you". You see, fear also means reverence and awe which is-- 'fear of the Lord'. By acting in faith and casting our fears on Him, we are transferring the anxiety to Him and He can handle it. He instructs us to "not be anxious about anything, but in everything by prayer and petition, with thanksgiving, present your requests to God. And the peace of God, which transcends all understanding, will guard your hearts and your minds in Christ Jesus". (Phil 4.6,7)

Our peace (absence of fear) in the midst of trials comes from understanding and trusting in the love of God for His children. That's YOU!!! Paul makes a bold and expansive statement about this in Rom 8.38,39. My abridged version is: "absolutely nothing can separate us from the love of God in Christ Jesus". See, fear is the debilitating enemy, not that of which we are fearful. One devastatingly false belief by many is that we are immune to trials and sufferings as Believers. Luke quotes Paul in Lk 14.22b that "we must enter the kingdom of God through many hardships". They are, in fact, God's crucible for our growth. Embrace it as Paul did. (Read II Cor 12.7-10)

How do I move from fearful to faithful? By prayerfully believing – He will sustain you—He will never let you fall—He cares for you—He will give you His peace. My problem, and maybe yours, is that I cast the cares on Him, but I keep reeling them back in. So, then, what I do is simply cast them back again till I get tired of reeling (and start resting).

Take hold of His word, stand on its promises, look fear in the face and claim the shed blood of Jesus! Grace will abound! And this way, you shoo away all the 'ghosts' in your life. And what God said to Jacob in Isa 43.1b, He says to us; "Fear not, for I have redeemed you; I have summoned you by name; you are mine."

DAY 17 | *Doves*

*D*OVE….is a species of the pigeon. Now, all you dove hunters, who knew that? They are stout-bodied birds. And before going further, it is related to the extinct 'dodos'. Pronounced, doughdoughs, dodo! They are worldwide but some areas are overrun with them. In the south, dove season is normally in the Fall. That's when men become men! Well, not all of us. The cooing is simply soothing to the ears. They seem so far away, but yet they are close by. Sort of like 'aviary ventriloquists'. I have observed they most often run in pairs. Thus, in The Twelve Days of Christmas lyrics; two turtledoves…

In ancient times most built their untidy nests in clefts of rocks as mentioned in S of Solomon 2.14. But Dovey, and mate, pictured here, built hers on the top of the outdoor ceiling fan on the porch at my daughter's home. Orders were given; no one turns on the fan till they're gone. Sure enough, all proceeded as Dovey planned and new dovettes were hatched. Of all of the birds in God's creation, I think it is one of the most lovely in shape, color and temperament.

Primarily, most people relate them with peace, or the loving turtledoves. Politically, the terms hawks and doves come to mind.   Research shows the dove is symbolic of Biblical and literary expressions. In Christian art…

- it symbolizes the Holy Ghost/Spirit
- in church windows the seven rays signify the seven gifts of the Spirit
- and the human soul, represented as coming out of the mouth of saints at death
- Holy Spirit descending on Jesus at His baptism as a dove

Biblically, there are many ways the dove is depicted and used in God's plan of redemption.

- the dove was sent out by Noah three times to see if the land was dry-Gen 8.8-12
- God called for a turtledove and pigeon at His covenant with Abram-Gen 15.9-10
- a young dove or pigeon was used by priests in burnt offerings of birds-Lev 1.14

And in the baptism of Jesus, the dove plays a significant role for all that were present and as a testimony for future generations. Then John (the Baptist) gave this testimony: "I saw the Spirit come down from heaven as a dove and remain on Him. I would not have known Him, except that the One who sent me to baptize with water told me, the Man on whom you see the Spirit come down and remain is He who will baptize with the Holy Spirit. I have seen and testify that this is the Son of God". Luke's account is in 3.21,22. "..Jesus was baptized too. And as He was praying, heaven was opened and the Holy Spirit descended on Him in bodily form like a dove. And a voice came from heaven: "You are My Son, whom I love; with You I am well pleased.""

Oddly, at 24, the last dove I ever shot fell at my feet half alive, cooing and blinking those piercing black eyes at me. Like the priests at the sacrifice, I had to wring his neck as an act of mercy. I have never hunted since that moment.

Now, when I think of my experience it reminds me of the merciful sacrifice Jesus made for me, shedding His precious blood, symbolized by the sacrificial doves in the Old Testament. And when *The Dove* descended at His baptism, He was, in essence, empowering Him to make the eventual sacrifice of His own blood for us.

God speaks volumes to us in His creation. Are we listening? Do we even care? The next time you hear the cooing, or see two love birds on a limb; be reminded of Jesus' and His Father's love for you. Maybe you might even 'coo' back to Him in grateful praise.

DAY 18 | *Robins*

ROBINS….are, in a manner of speaking, the official usherers of Spring in most parts of North America. At least where I have lived. The two just seem to go together. And who has not sung, or at least heard, the little ditty-- 'when the red, red robin comes bob, bob, bobbing along'. The writer must have observed their actions as this is just what they do when moving along the ground. As with migratory birds, the males return around March to their summer breeding grounds before the females, and compete with each other for nesting sites. During the breeding season, the adult males grow distinctive black feathers on their heads; after the season they lose this eye-catching plumage. Sorta like a lot of us guys, especially in later years. Listen to this, men; the female then selects a mate based on his song and the desirability of the nests he has built. Pretty smart, ladies!

While dining one early evening on Mother's Day on an outdoor patio, my daughter noticed a robin in a nest of a nearby tree in a cradle of the lower branches. The male and female were flying in and out seeking worms (to each his own) to feed their newborns. We and many others gathered around the tree and observed nature at its best. They were not in the least frightened or distracted from their mission. What I want to know is how do they know where the worms are? Someone suggested that they can hear them. Maybe more research is needed.

Just then, Annie, my youngest granddaughter, rushed up to me exclaiming that this was a wonderful opportunity for my next 'LSTU'. What we saw and experienced was a responsible family providing their newborns with the provisions for life. Fulfilling the task for which God had made them. Creating, providing and extending… life. But the most compelling lesson was the complete dependency and trust of the baby 'robinettes'. Still blind, safely in the nest, under the comfort of mother's wings; and when food arrived, heads turned skyward with wide open mouths chirping to high heaven. What a spiritual moment! Close your eyes and imagine or just look at the photo we took.

Scripture shouts of this to us. Psalm 150 sings aloud "praise God in His sanctuary". And in 126.2, "then our mouth was filled with laughter and our tongue with singing".   The Psalmist goes on- "To thee I lift up my eyes, O You that are enthroned in the heavens! Behold, as the eyes of servants look to the hand of their masters, as the eyes of a maiden to the hand of her mistress; so our eyes look to the Lord our God". (Psa. 123.1,2) We are exhorted in 134.2 to "lift up our hands in the sanctuary and bless the Lord". You see, the robins are doing just that in the sanctuary God provided them. Their song, their obedience, their work, their trust; all is a 'joyful noise to the Lord'.   I simply cannot get the image of the babies out of my mind; laid back, mouths skyward and wide open. Have you ever thought of worshipping like that? So utterly helpless and so very dependent.

Finally, I am reminded of Jesus' words in Mt 6.26 when discussing God's provisions. "Look at the birds of the air, they do not sow, neither do they reap, nor gather into barns; and yet your heavenly Father feeds them. Are you not worth much more than they?" He later in 8.20 reminds us "the foxes have holes and the birds of the air have nests; but he Son of God has no where to lay His head". See, Jesus knows our needs far greater than we. And He asks us to "seek Him first and His righteousness, and all the things we need, will be added to us". (Mt 6.33) Sounds like the robins have it figured out much better than we. So, heads up, hands lifted; open wide, singing praises in your sanctuary and trust that His provisions are adequate for the task(s) He has given you. And one last thing; He promises if "His own ask for a fish, He will not give them a snake, will He"? (Mt 7.10) The little robin knows that; do we?

Bob, bob, bob on over and let's share robin stories.

DAY 19 | *Lion*

*L*ION...the reputed king of the jungle, at least the male. I know, I watched Lion King several times already. Many think it is the beast to be most feared. Ask its potential prey! Swift, powerful, patient, proud and fearless. A large, heavily built social cat. Social? I agree with the large and heavily built. Sounds more like a Hollywood leading man than a ferocious beast.

The circus trainers make them look so tame, sorta like pussy cats. A whip and a chair just doesn't seem adequate to me. Zoos, that's another story. Iron bars make them appear harmless and us, brave. The roar tells another story. In the open jungle, his habitat, it must send chills through all living things in hearing distance. Am I his target?

Daniel was thrown in a lion's den and survived. Sampson, and David, as young men, slew lions, primarily with their bare hands.   The Old Testament is filled with examples of lion cubs, lions and lionesses; mostly related to fierce or deadly activity. We all have observed a cat crouch low in the grass or weeds, with the ears and eyes laid back, waiting to spring for the 'kill'. David in Psalm 17.12 explains to God that his enemies "are like a lion hungry for prey, like a great lion crouching in cover".

And in Genesis, God speaks with Cain concerning his disobedience. And he likens sin to the lion in Psalms. "...And if you do not do well, sin is crouching at the door; and its desire is for you..." (Gen 4.7b) He finishes by saying "...but you must master it." Think on this. Sin is the king of the jungle in which we live. Satan uses it to consume/defeat us. Alone, Daniel, Sampson and David would have been devoured. The Spirit of the Lord was present in every one of these instances. Would you go lion hunting with a switch? Not on your life. But for many of us, that is what we are doing and we're open prey for the enemy. Most are simply unaware of the powerful grip sin has on us.

Peter warns us. "Be of sober spirit, be on the alert. Your adversary, the devil, prowls about like a roaring lion, seeking someone to devour." (I Pet 5.8) But, in Him, we can resist, overcome; even be victorious. "..because greater is He who is in you than he who is in the world." (I Jn 4.4b) Lions are not to be toyed with and so not sin.   We are not able, but Revelation 5.5 gives us the confidence to face our sins and the enemy. "Then one of the elders said to me, 'Do not weep! See, the Lion of the tribe of Judah, the root of David, has triumphed.'" Jesus is that Lion, that 'root'. He was there slaying David's lion and He's here to slay ours through His Spirit. The same Spirit of the Lord who came upon Samson in power to slay his lion. And the same God who sent His angel to shut the mouth of the lions for Daniel.

"Let us draw near to God with a sincere heart in full assurance of faith.." (Heb 10.22a) Identify the 'lions' in your life, call upon Him in faith and together you will be victorious.

I've never been lion or big game hunting but it sounds scary and exciting, both at the same time. Maybe it is frighteningly similar to walking by faith. Check your spiritual pulse. Is it racing, even a little bit? If not, maybe you don't realize you are in the hunt. Or even worse, that 'you' are the prey.

I am certain there are 'stories' you have when you faced a bear or lion, your gun jammed and you survived with your bare hands (or fast feet). Shoot them on over and we'll roar together.

DAY 20 | *Moon*

$\mathcal{T}$he MOON…is the natural satellite of the Earth. Man has always been fascinated by this orbiting sphere in our universe. So many images, so many songs, so much folklore has been linked to the Moon. Has anyone seen the 'man in the moon'? August or Harvest Moon, Blue Moon; the list is endless. Wolves howl at the Moon, voyagers track it, scientists and astronomers study it. Astronauts travel to the Moon (first one in 1969); some have even walked on it. Many marriage proposals have been spoken under the moon's glow. The Bible addresses the New Moon for seasons of worship.

It simply sits there orbiting the Earth about every four weeks and the Earth only sees one side. The 'dark side' never faces us. The Moon has no light of its own but is a 'reflector' of the sun's brilliant rays. From the early crescent to the full disclosure, it is all there but the shadow of the Earth and the angle of the sun create the various shapes. The gravitational attraction that the Moon exerts on the Earth is the cause of tides on the sea. Tidal flow is synchronized to the Moon's orbit around the Earth. I accept this; I simply don't understand it.

"The heavens declare the glory of God and the firmament shows His handiwork…" (Psa 19.1) Clearly, His majestic nature can be witnessed, simply by gazing at one of His masterpieces, the Moon. But what does it have to say to us? We are much like the Moon. Unto ourselves, we are less than useful. No radiance of our own. In fact, we are more like the 'dark side'. Our works are as 'filthy rags'; 'there is none righteous, no not one'. The Moon goes about its business from day to day, always being in the right spot for the given moment. Actually, it is obedient to God's commands. That is why the sun can perform its task of reflecting the light off the moon. The moon simply is the conduit, not the source of light.

And so are we. John tells us in v. 1.9 "that (Jesus) was the true Light which gives light to every man who comes into the world". Isa 2.5 exhorts us. "O house of Jacob, come and let us walk in the light of the Lord." Paul exclaims in Eph 5.8—"You were once darkness, but you now are light in the Lord. Walk as children of light…" The moon would be in total darkness, not just half of it, if it were not for the sun's light.

Paul goes on to say that "the fruit of the Spirit is in all goodness, righteousness and truth". None of these attributes exist in unredeemed man. So, until the Son, through His Spirit, shines in and through us, we are like the sunless moon. No light, no radiance.

Since Jesus is the 'true Light', and we are 'the light of the world' it would make sense that we are not the source, only conduits or reflectors of the 'True Light'. "I am crucified with Christ, nevertheless I live, yet not I, but Christ lives in me; and the life I now live in the flesh, I live by faith in the Son of God, who loved me and gave Himself for me." (Gal 2.20) So, as the moon is obedient to God's laws and continues its orbiting, so we must, through faith, continue our obedience so the Son may shine through us to a dark world. "…a city that is set on a hill cannot be hidden. Nor do they light a lamp and put it under a basket, but on a lampstand, and it gives light to all that are in the house. Let your light so shine before men, that they may see your good works and glorify your Father in heaven." (Mt 5.14b-16)

All of us love the full moon. Anything less is caused by something blocking the sun's rays; that is, the Earth. We too want to be a 'full light' for Him. The sin and disobedience in our lives diminish the glory of the Son in our lives. So, in order for us to shine brightly for Him, we need to remove the obstacles that mar the image. Then, we too can be a 'full moon' of God's 'goodness, righteousness and truth' to the world.

The next time you look at the Moon, reflect on the True Source of its light.

DAY 21 | *Angels*

ANGELS…do you believe in them? More so, have you ever wrestled with one? Well, I have; and, fortunately, he won! Our young family was in Crested Butte, back when I was a poor skier; now I'm a non-skier. Don't get me wrong, I love Colorado, the majestic mountains and regal beauty.

We were scheduled to leave the slopes soon to head for the airport. But I pushed the envelope and decided to make a couple more runs. Bad idea! About halfway down the first run, suddenly out of nowhere, I fell. Like someone had pushed me. One of my skis came completely off, including the bindings. It was a few feet away, and as I would reach for it, the ski would move farther out of my reach. As I struggled to recover it, maybe 2-3 minutes, I had the sense that I needed to get off the hill and head for home, foregoing the next run(s). And that is when the realization hit me—I've been in the grip of an angel of God. There simply was no other explanation. I sensed a release, secured the stray ski, and made the way home. I told the family the story—there had to be a reason for it. We barely made our flight (pre-security checks).

Upon arriving home I had an urgent call. The father of one our young friends in our sport's circle had died suddenly. She simply adored him and at the time he was her basketball coach. I, along with her pastor, stepped in that day as her source of consolation, and for the remainder of the season, we coached her team and became the go-to men in her life. She went on to play college soccer and became an ordained Methodist minister. It became apparent. God simply wanted me back in Dallas that day and He sent an angel to ensure it happened.

That's a nice story Bill, but what does that have to do with me? AWARENESS!!! I found 276 references to angel(s) in the Bible; from Genesis to Revelation. Among other things, they visit, bring messages, make announcements, guard the saints, open jail doors, represent God, destroy armies, roll back stones and much more.

Look at your life. If you are like me, I have innumerable situations I cannot explain. I should be dead several times—miraculous events kept me alive, even untouched. Angels are there—for you and me. Heb 13.2 exhorts us… "Do not forget to entertain strangers, for by so doing some people have entertained angels without knowing it". Our prayers give God's angels power for victory over the evil realm. PRAY DAILY that God's host of angels will guard you and your family. Name them and pray a hedge of protection around them. Don't raise your family by chance...but by choice—choosing to invoke the presence of all God's heavenly host each day.

I challenge you to read and meditate on Daniel 10. In vs. 12 the angel said "Do not be afraid, Daniel. Since the first day that you set your mind to gain understanding and to humble yourself before your God, your words were heard, and I have come in response to them". Do you desire God's help and for Him to hear you? Then do as Daniel…1) set your mind to gain understanding and 2) humble yourself before God. But be careful, you just may invoke the presence of all kinds of strange events, maybe even an angelic visit. Hopefully, he won't have to wrestle with you to get your attention.

What do you think? Had any circumstances or visitations you can't explain?

DAY 22 | *Streams*

$\mathcal{S}$ TREAMS...are natural bodies of flowing water on or under the earth. Babbling brooks, creeks (cricks in some parts); all conjure up some visions in our minds from past experiences. Especially when we were young or our trips to the mountains. Fly fishermen, canoers or rafters, explorers have the best views and visual memories. Commercials highlight 'Rocky Mountain" streams. Magazines treat us with visuals of streams and many golf courses are designed around them. Serenity, rest, freshness, life--all come to mind.

Some flow smoothly with only a slight ripple while others rush through rocks and boulders and over waterfalls. Most embody both. The higher elevations provide the coldest temperatures; and quite naturally are most times the most brilliant. Fish can be seen swimming with the flow while salmon at times swim upstream, battling the odds to return to their original home. Trout, crappie, brim, catfish, stripers and more. The sun glistening off the ripples and the sound; a pleasure to both the eyes and ears. Have you ever just stood and gazed, or cupped your hands and drank the fresh clear water?

Scripture speaks of streams. David took five smooth stones from a stream to use as a weapon against Goliath. Psa 1 is descriptive of "a man whose delight is in the law of the Lord, and who meditates on it day and night". It tells us "he will be like a tree planted by streams, yielding fruit, his leaf not withering and prospering". The Psalmist worships with a familiar image; "And as a deer pants for streams of water, my soul pants for you". (Psa 42.1) Amos chimes in—"But let justice roll on like a river, righteousness like a never-failing stream". (5.24)

The steams are flowing downhill to their eventual destination. Solomon tells us "All streams flow into the sea.." (Ecc 1.7a) And on their way they provide life to plants, trees, animals, fish, mammals, birds and people. Jesus summed it up so well and so profoundly with this. "Whoever believes in Me, as the Scripture has said, streams of living water will flow from him." (Jn 7.38) That 'living water' is the Holy Spirit which He has given us who believe.

It has been my observation that the clearest, freshest, purest water is found in streams where sand, pebbles, rocks and boulders exist. The water rushes over, against and through them, being purified along the way. Is this not a picture of us? On our way to heaven and eventually into the presence of the Lord, we encounter many obstacles, like the stream, that are there for our sanctification, and not to harm us. God uses these to cleanse us, equip us and prepare us. Embrace them, thank Him for them and flow through them. And as we go, God will use us to provide hope, strength, wisdom and an abundant life to others along the way.

The next stream you come to; stop, ponder and meditate on Him. Guaranteed to refresh!!

*B*EES…what in the world can they tell us? There's a recent movie I watched with my grandkids entitled the 'Bee Movie'. While watching, I was struck by the message that was coming through. Besides being funny, serious and containing a message, it was also entertaining.

What most people relate with bees is their sting, something to avoid at all costs. It is a special species (over 20,000) of the wasp. And who wants to make friends with a wasp. Never met one I'd trust. And then there is the honey thing, flowers and pollen. Can you imagine how much work it takes to fill up one of those bear-shaped honey jars on the grocery shelf? The most common is the European honey bee, the bumble bee and the stingless bee (now there's a bee we all can embrace).

Everything about the bee is primarily for intensive labor in the world of pollenization. The 'queen' bee rules! So, what's new about that? Her sisters are the worker bees, and then we have the Drone. You guessed it-the male (comes from an unfertilized egg). Chosen to fertilize a receptive queen and die. At least he gets out of all the work. A typical hive may have 60,000 female worker bees. All interested in the latest buzz around the hive. (UGGHH). Get to the message, Bill.

The bee's sole mission in life is to bring pollen back to the hive to make honey. This activity is necessary for them to sustain life. It is the way they serve and please the queen. And the same with us. Our sole purpose as Believers is to bring praise and honor to God through His Son in the power of the Holy Spirit. Paul says it well in Romans 12.1. "Therefore, I urge you, brothers, in view of God's mercy, to offer your bodies as living sacrifices, holy and pleasing to God – this is your spiritual act of worship." As the queen equips her workers, so God "equips us for every good work". (II Tim 3.17) And like a worker bee, "I call to the Lord, who is worthy of praise." (Psa 18.3)

--The buzz is our praise; the word is the pollen; the honey is the fruit of the Spirit—

Psalms 19.10b shows us that God's word is "sweeter also than honey and the honeycomb". As hard and as effectively the bees work producing sweet honey, scripture tells us God's word is better and sweeter to our life. Colossians 1.10 sums it up. "And we pray this in order that you may live a life worthy of the Lord and may please Him in every way; bearing fruit in every good work, growing in the knowledge of God, being strengthened with all power according to His glorious might so that you may have great endurance and patience, and joyfully giving thanks to the Father who has qualified you to share in the inheritance of the saints in the kingdom of light."

The next time you encounter a bee; instead of dodging 'her', remember, she is just serving her queen the only way she can—and be reminded of your relationship to Him.

And that His Son took the sting for us on the cross!

DAY 24 | *Crib*

CRIB…is something that projects for most of us modern city folk a single visual image when we hear the word… a child's bed with enclosed sides. Most are neat and tidy, with warm blankets and lots of toys. Some are stationery, some portable, some old ones actually rock. Many are 'hand me downs' from generations past; very special. Fond memories, accompanied by many strange faces and sounds like googoo, dada, mama, gootchy gootchy goo. Pictures galore!! And, of course, periodic odors and nasty aftermaths. But for the most part, a joyous part of family life. What a safe environment to spend the early part of one's life.

But for some people in this world, a crib has an entirely different meaning. A stall or pen for cattle or horses; a rack or manger for fodder, as in a stable or barn. Hay or straw is the prevalent content, which provides a bed or makes an eating trough, or both. Insects, lice, dirt and dust accompany most cribs. Did I mention they are typically open and airy? Not the first place into which you and I would think of to place our newborn.

Christmas came over 2,000 years ago, and it had its beginning in the latter crib. Let's ponder why the Very God of the Universe, the Great I Am, would allow His only Son to start this way? I'm an only child and I was born in a house during a Tennessee snow storm. So why did even I have it better than Jesus? We're not talking about a God that could not afford the best, a crib for royalty, a 'hand me down' kind. He owns all of creation. We dwell in the "Inn of God".

Make no mistake; the place was not a mistake!!! Just as the cross was not one either. Certainly, it had been prophesied long before. It was an intentional plan. Micah 5.2 was written 700+ years earlier. "But you Bethlehem Ephrathah, though you are little among the thousands of Judah, yet out of you shall come forth to Me the One to be ruler in Israel, whose goings forth have been from old, from everlasting." Just as the small village was not an afterthought, some alternative locale, neither was the meager bed of birth. Jesus came as the 'suffering servant' (Lk 24.26), as the 'good shepherd' (Jn 10.11). He will return as a 'triumphant King' (Rev 19.16). But that is another story. He came to save the lost (Mt 19.11) and heal the sick (Mt 9.12), not dwell in royal palaces. His birthplace and crib demonstrate the profoundest of messages to the world. God can relate to us in the lowest of our circumstances. He simply demonstrated humility of the highest order, right from the beginning of His Son's earthly life.

Phil 2.5-11 sums it up best. A crib to glory set of verses. "Have this attitude in yourselves which was also in Christ Jesus, who, although He existed in the form of God, did not regard equality with God a thing to be grasped, but emptied Himself, taking the form of a bond-servant, and being made in the likeness of men. And being found in appearance as a man, He humbled Himself by becoming obedient to the point of death, even death on a cross. Therefore also God highly exalted Him, and bestowed on Him the name which is above every name, that at the name of Jesus every knee should bow, of those who are in heaven, on earth, and under the earth, and that every tongue should confess that…Jesus Christ is Lord, to the glory of God the Father."

CHRIST IS BORN!!! HALLELUJAH!!!

This year, look deeply into each manger scene, ponder God's love for you, right from the start. He placed no relational barrier between us and Him. A Master-ful plan!! We call it ……………………………………

Christmas!

Also, have a worship-filled, servant-hearted Christmas like none you have ever experienced! For it all started this way at His cribside.

GOLF......(you had to know it was coming sooner or later) has long been a recreational pleasure of mine. I coined it to mean..'game *of lazy fellers*'. Legend would confirm this; as it is suggested that bored shepherds near St. Andrews, Scotland became adept at hitting rounded stones into rabbit holes with their wooden crooks. Boys will be boys! (My personal apologies to those who could give a rip about golf.)

As I play I often think of the similarities to 'real life' in so many ways. I have had the distinct joy of helping Luke, my eldest grandson, learn the game. And we have played each week for almost 2 years as he was homeschooling. He's quite good. We've discussed the game of golf and life. Hope some of it took.

As in life, one must have the basic, correct fundamentals; the tools to perform at a certain level. It starts with the grip, the stance, ball position, takeaway, the swing thru the ball, the follow thru, and the knowledge of the rules.

Good fundamentals-vital to success in any endeavor

Operating within the rules of the game-that's the way we must play

Love for the game-enjoying what you do and those you serve

Focus on the task at hand

While there are many lessons from the game, there is one I would like to address…focus on 'staying in the present'. I heard this term from Tiger Woods a few years ago. In an interview, he said he worked hard at doing just that. So, Tiger, what do you mean? I think the Scriptures can answer for him. Mt 6.34 (NIV) says "therefore do not worry about tomorrow, for tomorrow will worry about itself. Each day has enough trouble of its own".

We live in 'time'. There is past, present and future. The last shot is over, it is history, it is 'past'. The present shot is the one we have to deal with. It is always changing, depending on what the past shot created. The future or next shot has not taken place. So don't worry about either the past or the future shots, but as the Word teaches us, there is enough trouble right in front of you that needs all the focus and energy possible to execute well.

Have you ever missed an easy putt (I have), become angry, then step up to the tee box and as you are still lathering over the last putt, find you are so up tight, you hit a poor drive. The past failure dictated the present. And how do I operate within my trials which might dictate my future and have the peace to deal with the present? The Bible suggests; "Do not be anxious for anything, but in everything, by prayer and petition, with thanksgiving, present your requests to God. And the peace of God, which transcends all understanding, will guard your hearts and minds in Christ Jesus." (Phil 4.6, 7) Casting is a bad thing in a golf swing, but in life, I find it to be the only way I can stay in the moment and not be dragged down over the issues of which I have no control. When I don't, anxiety prevails. Two verses in the Bible address this very clearly. Psa 55.22.."Cast your cares on the Lord and He will sustain you; He will never allow the righteous to fall." And I Pet 5.7; "Cast all your anxiety on Him because He cares for you".

Trust is the substance that allows you and me to act on the above. Unlike golf, where the caddy tells us to 'trust our swing'; our trust is in the all-loving and all-sufficient Lord, who is able to accomplish what He has promised. Simply put; there just is no other alternative; that is, if you want to be effective by 'staying in the present'. Thanks, Tiger, for showing us that the game played in the present is far more productive and rewarding. I'd say his credentials speak to its effect.

What are you dealing with right now that needs to be 'cast on the Lord' so you may stay in the present with peace and not anxiety?

DAY 26 | *Sheep*

$\mathcal{S}$ HEEP…are an interesting cud-chewing mammal group. First, they are born to be sheared. Some of us experience this (fleeced) without it being our life's call. Did you know they are related to the goat but stockier? A timid, defenseless creature, noted for its flesh and wool. Plus the word is both singular and plural.   By definition, they are easily influenced and led. Research showed at least 15 breeds. The male sheep do not have beards like the goat. (and most are one gatepost short of a fence)

Oh, does scripture have a lot to say about them! With many comparisons to us humans. God knew what He was doing when He created us both. I guess it is mostly our similar tendencies. Lost as sheep; dumb as sheep; and others come to mind. But rarely a compliment. They stray off by themselves, get caught in fences and thickets, can't get up when they are on their back; all of which make them easy prey for wild animals. The shepherd, his dog and the crooked staff are so necessary for a sheep's survival.

The initial truth in Isa 53.6 makes the most chilling comparison.   "All we like sheep have gone astray; we have turned, everyone, to his own way…". This deadly characteristic in us drove our Shepherd to the cross. And what a Shepherd; "I lay down my life for the sheep". (Jn 10.15b) He knows, left alone, we are open prey for the devil. The love of God is so deep and is revealed in the Parable of the Lost Sheep in Lk 15.4, 5. "What man of you, having a hundred sheep, if he loses one of them, does not leave the ninety-nine in the wilderness, and go after the one that is lost until he finds it. And when he has found it, he lays it on his shoulders, rejoicing." REJOICING!! Did you get that?

Sheep recognize a single voice. They respond to it. "…and the sheep hear his voice; and he calls his own sheep by name and leads them out. And when he brings out his own sheep, he goes before them; and the sheep follow him, for they know his voice." (Jn 10.3, 4) They are absolutely content to be in his control. Why not? David explains why in the beginning of the 23rd Psalm. "The Lord is my shepherd, I shall not want, He makes me to lie down in green pastures, He leads me beside still waters, He restores my soul.." And later; "Surely goodness and mercy shall follow me all the days of my life, and I shall dwell in the house of the Lord forever". Left to themselves, sheep simply can not find that which sustains their life. But under the shepherd's care, it has nothing to want for. It is all provided.

Psa 100.8 is comforting. "We are His people and the sheep of His pasture." Can't you sense the peace of a flock of sheep lying down in the pasture with water nearby? And sensing the presence of their shepherd. "Be anxious for nothing, but in everything, by prayer and supplication, with thanksgiving, let your requests be made known unto God, and the peace that passes all understanding will guard your heart and mind in Christ Jesus." (Phil 4.6, 7) Are you trying to be the shepherd in your life, when all He asks is that we be His sheep, listen for His voice, and follow Him? Psa 46.10a sums it up.

"BE STILL (little sheep) AND KNOW THAT I AM GOD!"

To all those herdsmen out there, give me a 'bleep' at your convenience and spin your woolly story.

*R*AINBOW…an arc or circle in the sky caused by the refraction of the sun's rays by rain or clouds. Most of us quickly think about the proverbial 'pot of gold' at the foot of the rainbow. Fishermen reflect on the Rainbow trout flashing their multi-colors through a clear mountain stream. Songs have been written about 'chasing rainbows'. The seven colors in a spectrum are something we learn early as a child. Can you name them all? They are red, orange, yellow, green, blue, indigo, violet. The same effect as a rainbow can be accomplished when a beam of white light is dispersed when passing through a prism. Each color is bent, red the most and violet the least.

On a recent road trip my daughter and her son were confronted by a magnificent double rainbow. After stopping and gazing for several minutes, and numerous photos later (one is shown here), they were simply awestruck by the beauty and clarity of colors. But it was not the rainbow as much as it was the God who allowed it to be placed there for all to view.

Based on my Bible research, only three places address rainbows, with only one, Gen 9.13-17, actually discussing the one in the sky. The other references are in Ezek 1.27,28 and Rev 4.1-3 and 10.1. These refer to the surrounding radiance, as the likeness of the glory of the Lord. Appropriate, I would think. But in Genesis we see and hear what God says to Noah. "I set My rainbow in the cloud, and it shall be for the sign of the covenant between Me and the earth. It shall be, when I bring a cloud over the earth, that the rainbow shall be seen in the cloud; and I will remember My covenant which is between Me and you and every living creature of all flesh; the waters shall never again become a flood to destroy all flesh. The rainbow will be in the cloud, and I will look on it to remember the everlasting covenant between God and every living creature of all flesh that is on the earth. And God said to Noah, 'this is the sign of the covenant which I have established between Me and all flesh that is on the earth.'"

God made numerous covenants with His people. The last one was the covenant in His Son's blood for salvation. Jesus said in Luke 22.20 and elsewhere in the Gospels; "This cup is the new covenant in My blood, which is shed for you". All of God's covenants are about 'salvation'. While most can not be viewed, the one signified by the rainbow can. The rainbow is the sign of the first one, with Noah and his descendants, and guess what, that is you and me. What do covenants entail? Well, for starters; promise, oath, commitment, pledge, contract—legal and binding on the party. No backsliding, no appeals court. He is the 'Supreme Court'. If God is the same 'yesterday, today and forever', then how would we ever question the authenticity of His covenant promises?

When it starts flooding in your area, do you ever think that the whole earth will once again be covered? I don't, and I bet you don't either. Why? He promised. Then why doubt the all-sufficiency of the gospel message: 'Christ died for our sins and rose from the dead'. It is a covenant made in His own blood on the cross that gives us, those who have trusted in Jesus alone, salvation. And just maybe there really is a 'pot of gold' at the end of every rainbow. I would attest that it is 'much more'! One of many verses addressing this come to my mind. Lk 12.28 tells us "If that is how God clothes the grass of the field, which is here today, and tomorrow is thrown into the fire, how much more will He clothe you, O you of little faith". So, the next time you see a rainbow in the clouds, marvel at the sight, but more so, marvel at the One who placed it there as a promise, and trust Him---in everything!

DAY 28 | *Clock*

*C*LOCK…used to measure time, in so many different ways. From nano-seconds to millinei. The new year 2009 is upon us. Only a few days left. And when it gets really close, we count down the seconds till the clock strikes midnight; a little celebration, after which time we start another 365 days. Then we don't watch the clock like we did moments earlier. Why is that? Life is filled with moments, some of which appear more special or significant than others.

Can some of you remember where you were when Neil Armstrong stepped on the moon, and his famous quote 'That's one small step for man-one giant leap for mankind'? Or the spot you occupied the day President John F. Kennedy was assassinated. And more recently, the destruction of the Twin Towers in New York on 9/11. The moment of birth of your first child or grandchild probably is indelibly etched in your mind.

We are locked into a space capsule where time is used to determine or measure almost everything we do. A one hundred meter sprinter or swimmer works countless hours just to take a split second off their time. No one wants the plane to be one minute late. Rush hour is not a rush hour, but a slow grind of endless delays and frayed nerves. Why, because it is making us late to something. And slow food service is truly the pits.

Not to mention a snail pace express lane in the grocery. These are only a few examples of how we are driven by the passing or, many times, the non-passage of time. Americans, if you want to add time to your day, just go to a Latin country. The clock has little meaning. There is no 'two minute warning' in Cuba.

The result of all the preoccupation with time is that we become dominated by the clock and filled with anxiety. Selfishness plays a big part too. I want what I want, and I want it now! God tells us "to be anxious for nothing, but in everything, by prayer and supplication, with thanksgiving, let your requests be made known unto God. And the peace of God, which passes all understanding, will guard your hearts and minds in Christ Jesus." (Phil 4.6, 7) Solomon in all his wisdom explains there is a time and season for everything. Mt 6.34 exhorts us to "take no thought for tomorrow….today has enough issues of its own". (my translation)

"Be still, and know that I am God." (Psa 46.10a) Thanks David, but how can I when the clock is running? When I yield my day, my moments, my life, I am saying to the Lord; You are in control of the time You have given me… to accomplish what You have chosen for me. In my life mission, the check-out line, traffic, my work day, with my spouse or kids, in a restaurant, at the airport. You get the point. Be still, calm down, take the foot off the petal, you are not in control. HE IS!!! Then time does not become our master, He does. Who created time; He did. Who controls the seasons and events; He does. When I forget this, self-centeredness takes over and once again I am back 'running my life' on 'my time schedule', which I never had under my control to begin with. And instead of enjoying 'peace that passes all understanding', I create anxiety that leads to disaster.

Maybe you have the same problem with managing time. Just remember, God created time, and He is still in control of it.

DAY 29 | *Violin*

*V*IOLIN ... an extraordinary instrument of fine music, originating from the basic fiddle, used to accompany singing and dancing. Being a Tennessee hillbilly, the Grand Ole Opry and its fiddlers were what I grew up loving. My maternal grandfather played one well. And as the saying goes, 'if you play music in Texas, you gotta have a fiddle in the band'. With maturity came the deep love for the violin and its unequaled musical splendor. From chamber music and solos to grand concert orchestras, the violin (the queen of instruments) leads the way.

Research reveals that most agree the first one was created by Andrea Amati about mid 1500's in Cremona, Italy. The Amati family taught Antonio Stradivari, who took it to its peak in artistic and acoustic perfection. Every violin wants to be an Amati or Stradivari. There are rare originals, ones with fake labels and fine copies. It is interesting that from four strings (and a bow), such quality of sound is achieved. It takes years of intense training and practice to master the violin, especially for concert level. Made out of four various woods, aged for years to perfection, it is crafted to produce a certain range of sounds. It is most beautiful when the artist and the violin become one.

Oddly, you and I are like these instruments. In the eyes of God, we are all Stradivaris. Right now, we may not sound like one, or have the beautiful finish, but God sees us as we are to become. Psa 119.73 tells it all. "Your hands have made me and fashioned me ..." Psalm 139 is a watershed chapter. Some things to ponder: "You formed my inward parts ... wove me in my mother's womb ... l am fearfully and wonderfully made ... my frame was not hidden from You when I was made in secret ..."

Amati saw and heard his creation, long before he completed it. You and I are being constructed with loving hands of the Master Craftsman and being fine tuned to fulfill our purpose. And what might that be? In the 150th Psalm we are being exhorted to "praise Him with lute and harp ... with stringed instruments and flutes ..." among other things. God-ordained creations such as a violin, are for our enjoyment but even more for His praise. Everything in His universe is ordained for His glory, and most definitely us, as we are 'made in His image'. As a Brother in Nashville often said; 'God don't make no junk'.

"God alone is worthy of praise." (Psa 18.3a) "It is His will for us that we should praise Him." (Psa 50.23a) We are being transformed into creatures who gratefully offer this praise to our Redeemer and God. " ... let everything that has breath praise the Lord." We are to praise Him for His creation, holiness, grace, goodness and kindness. Redeemed, being sanctified and on the road to becoming glorified beings (souls) should do it better than all others. The process of making us into His image is so similar to the development and refinement of the Stradivari violin. When completed, in the hands of The Great Artist, we become that for which we were intended.

Meanwhile, abuse and improper care for even a Stradivari renders it less than desirable for its purpose. Sin has had the same effect on us. Let us wipe off the dust (confess) and tune our strings (repent), so that we may, for eternity, PRAISE THE LORD!! And you don't have to be a master violinist to do that, and do it well. Let me hear of your musical tales of praise.

DAY 30 | *Shepherd's Prayer*

A SHEPHERD'S PRAYER…as captured in Psalm 23 is, to me, the crown jewel of scripture. There he is; the shepherd on the hillside with his herd of sheep. Night and day he and they have been together. A lot of time to think and ponder things in between all the bleeping. Sleeping under the stars, reflecting on the magnificence of God and His creation. Plus tending and observing the sheep in his care, reflecting on the similarities of man and sheep. Pondering the issues of life, reality of death, and the grace of God as it relates to it all. He's thinking, "Know that the Lord He is God, it is He that has made us and not we ourselves. We are His people and the sheep of His pasture." (Psa 100.3)

GRACE is all over these poetic phrases. I have recited this Psalm over a thousand times; in sadness, fear, joy and worship. And only recently has it been made so abundantly clear. The shepherd has cut through the chase, and nailed it. This is what I see as it relates to me, the sheep and Him, the Shepherd. Let's examine it.

I shall not want (for anything). Why? Five good reasons!

He is my Shepherd;
He makes me to lie down in green pastures;
He leads me beside still waters;
He restores (redeems) my soul;
He leads me down the paths of righteousness!

I shall walk fearlessly in the presence of evil and the shadow of death. Why? Six more!!

He is with me;
He provides comfort with His rod and staff;
He prepares a table for me in the very presence of my enemies;
He anoints my head with oil;
He provides a cup that overflows;
He blesses me with goodness and mercy all the days of my life! And to top it off—

I will dwell in His House, with Him, FOREVER!!!

Jesus said of Himself; "I am the Good Shepherd…..My sheep hear My voice". Lord, I hear your voice loud and clear, and I see the grace relationship with you as your sheep. I must admit this is a stacked deck in my favor.

In Him--1) my needs will be met; 2) I can walk in faith and not in fear of anything, not even death; 3) I get eternal life. All because I am His little lamb, HE does these eleven things for me, and more.

GRACE, PERSONIFIED!!!

So, some of you lambs might not sense this kind of relationship, and would like to.   Sheep know the voice of their shepherd, he leads and they follow him; because they trust him to care for them. In Psalm 23, the score is 11-3, in your favor. What a deal!! Make Jesus your SHEPHERD today! To better understand how, I would invite you to read the thoughts that follow this chapter. Sorta like a thirty-first day addition.

P.S. Psalm 23 would be a good health plan, would you agree? We could call it ShepherdCare!

SOURCE OF LIFE

Where to Start

Hopefully, you enjoyed reading these life messages and were challenged and blessed by all or some of the material But we should never lose sight of the overwhelming evidence that the Source/Author of all life is God, the Creator. His only Son, Jesus the Christ, was there in the beginning with the Father and the Holy Spirit. Old and New Testament scriptures speak clearly about the issue. In John 1. 3 the apostle tells us "All things came into being through Him (Son); and apart from Him nothing came into being that has come into being". He goes on to say in vs 4 that "In Him was life; and the life was the light of men".

And in Hebrews 1, parts of vss 1 and 2 tell us "God….in the last days has spoken to us in His Son, whom He appointed heir of all things, through whom also He made the world". Jesus said of Himself in John 14.6; "I am the way, and the truth and the life; no one comes to the Father, but through Me".

All of His creation speaks of His eternal qualities and majesty. We have but to gaze at the miracles of life each day to see it. Maybe for the first time, or in a deeper sense, you drew nearer to God through the moments you read and pondered on His word. Possibly, He spoke specifically to you, and there is now a desire to know Him more intimately. He said through His servant James in 4.8a that if you "draw near to God, and He will draw near to you". How do I do that?

According to I Corinthians 2, the gospel is: Christ died for our sins and rose from the dead. The following verses were the ones that led me to trust Christ.

Romans 3.23: "for all have sinned and fall short of the glory of God"

Romans 6.23: "for the wages of sin is death, but the free gift of God is eternal life in Jesus Christ our Lord"

Romans 5.8: "but God demonstrates His own love toward us, in that while we were yet sinners, Christ died for us"

Ephesians 2.8, 9: "for by grace you have been saved through faith; and that not of yourselves, it is the gift of God; not as a result of works, that no one should boast"

And in John 5.24 we see a truth that can be embraced through faith (trust) in Jesus who tells you and me… "Truly, truly, I say to you, he who hears My word, and believes Him who sent Me, <u>has</u> eternal life, and does not come into judgment, but has passed out of death into life." He spoke clearly again in John 11.25 when He said "I am the resurrection, and the life; he who believes in Me shall live even if he dies ".

If it is the desire of your heart to trust Jesus Christ for your salvation and to partake in His eternal life, then the following prayer would be a suggested way for you to take the step today. Read over the prayer and if it reflects your wishes, then pray it right now. Know that it is not the prayer that saves, but placing your trust in Christ alone for your salvation.

'Dear God, I know I'm a sinner. I know my sin deserves to be punished. I believe Christ died for me and rose from the grave. I trust Jesus Christ alone as my Savior. Thank you for the forgiveness and everlasting life I now have. In Jesus' name, amen.'

Welcome to the Kingdom of God! Did you hear the angels rejoicing? Well, they are!

Eternal life is based on fact, not feeling. Now…

1) Tell God what is on your mind through prayer-Philippians 4:6, 7
2) Read the Bible daily-II Timothy 3:16-17-Start in Philippians or John
3) Worship with God's people in a local church-Hebrews 10:24, 25
4) Tell others about Jesus Christ-Matthew 4:19

LaVergne, TN USA
15 April 2010
179277LV00001B